NEW WAY

Ben's bone and At the dentist

Illustrated by
Nina O'Connell

M
Macmillan Education

At the dentist

Fat Pig ran to the dentist.

He sat down with Ben.

Come in Jip, said the dentist.
What good teeth you have.
Here is a red toothbrush.

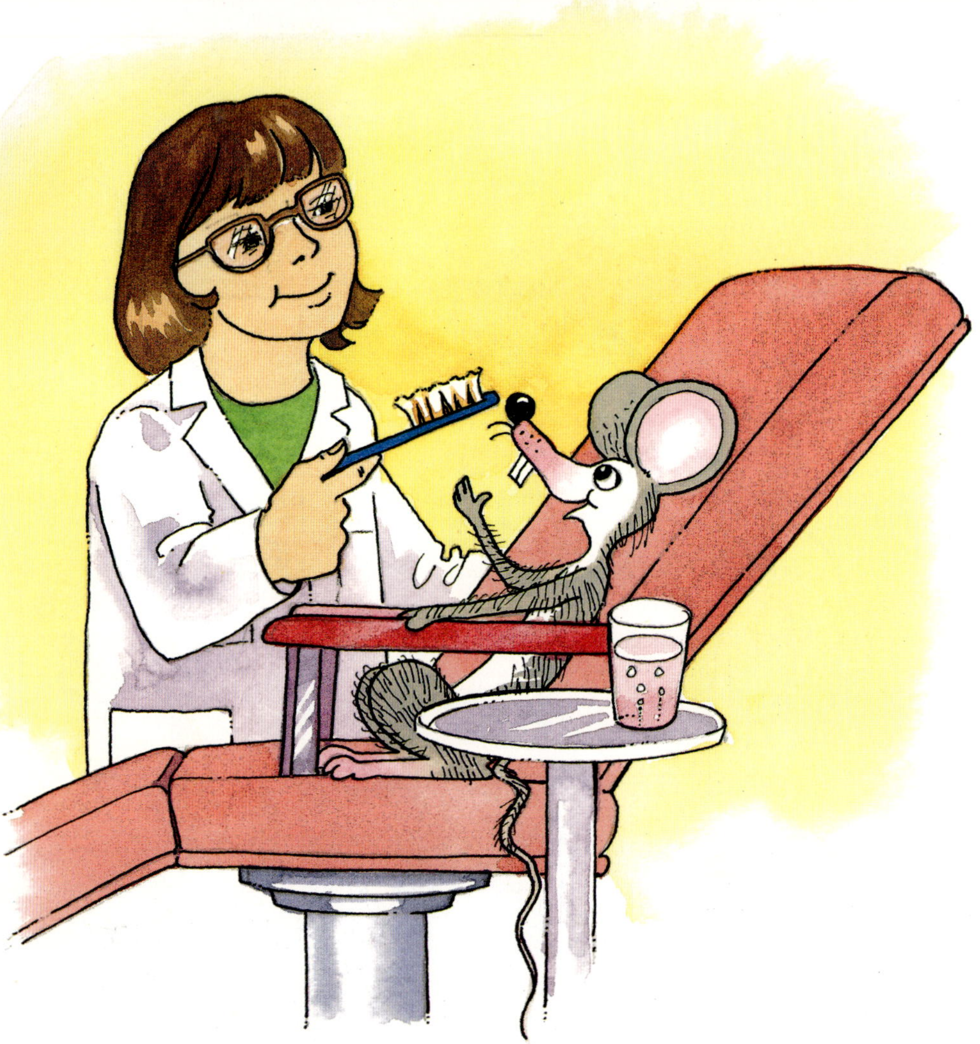

Come in Deb, said the dentist.
What long teeth you have.
Here is a blue toothbrush.

Come in Sam.
What big teeth you have Sam.
Here is a green toothbrush.

Come in Ben, said the dentist.
What strong teeth you have.
Here is a yellow toothbrush.

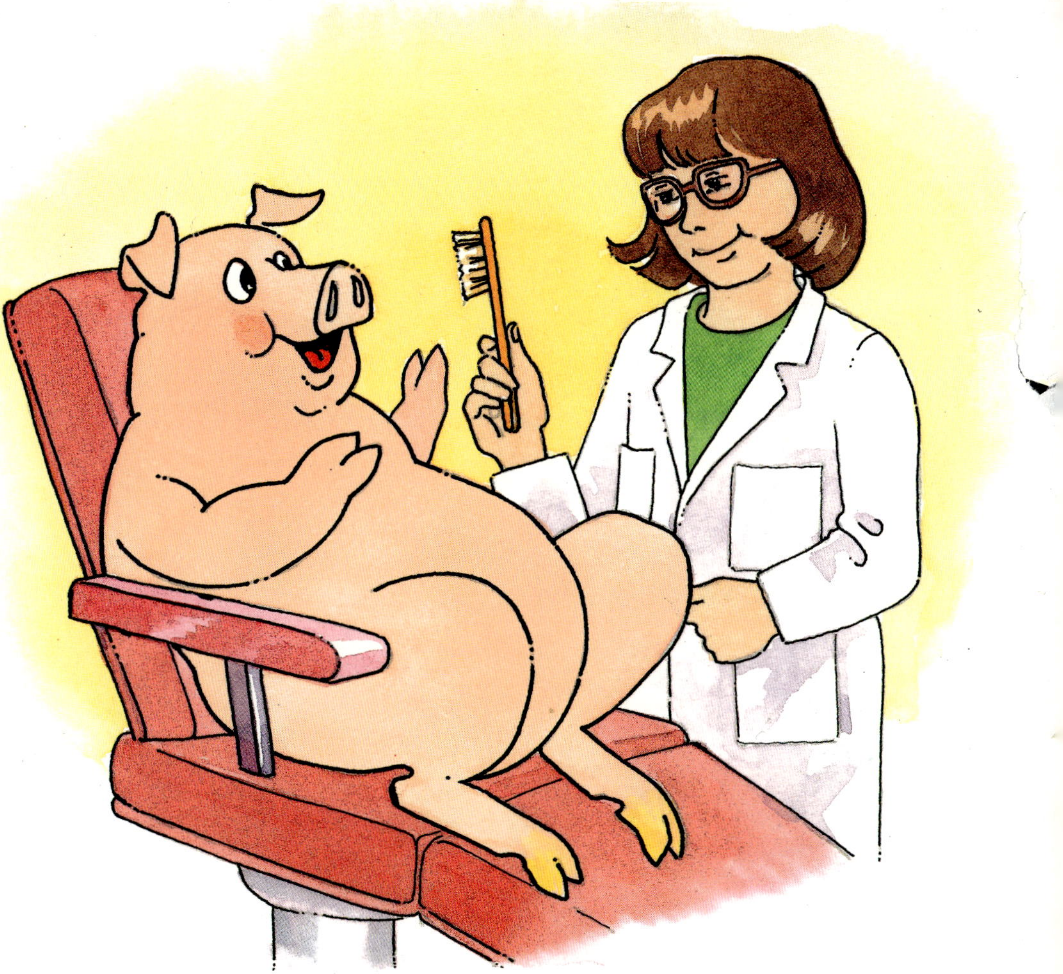

Come in Fat Pig, said the dentist.
Can I have a toothbrush,
said Fat Pig.
Yes you can, said the dentist.

You have no teeth Meg,
said Fat Pig.
Why do you want to see
the dentist.

Look what the dentist gave me,
said Meg.
She gave me a beak brush.

Ben's bone

Ben is sad.
He can not find his bone.
Is it a little bone,
said Jip.

No. It is a big bone,
said Ben.
I will look in my basket,
said Jip.

Is this your bone,
said Jip.
No. It is not my bone,
said Ben sadly.

Ben, Ben. Is this your bone,
said Deb.
No, said Ben.
I can't eat that bone.

Have you got Ben's bone,
said Sam.
Is this your bone,
said the man.
Oh yes. That looks like
my bone, said Ben.

I can't lift this bone,
said Ben.
Will you help me Meg.
No I won't, said Meg.
Will you help me Fat Pig.
No I won't, said Fat Pig.

I will help you, said Sam.
I like bones.